AF226125

The Adventures of Princess Zora and her Lightning Touch

Written by Dr. Cecily Anthony

Edited by Christine Barham, D. Phil.

Copyright 2021

Publisher CVC, LLC

Website: www.theadventuresofprincesszora.com

Email: cvc-llc@outlook.com

eBook ISBN: 978-0-578-84787-0
Hardcover ISBN: 978-0-578-84788-7

Illustrated by Suma at GetYourBookIllustrations
Cover design by GetYourBookIllustrations

"I have the nerve to walk my own way,
however hard, in my search for reality,
rather than climb upon the rattling wagon
of wishful illusions."
– *Zora Neale Hurston*

For Doralyn,
my beautiful gift.

Princess Zora
is six years old,
she is in Kindergarten,
and she lives with her
parents, King Zev
and Queen Zuri.

Princess Zora loves to read.

Princess Zora loves to
play with her dolls.

Princess Zora loves to play dress-up.

Princess Zora loves to draw beautiful pictures.

Princess Zora
loves to
play the piano.

Princess Zora
loves to
do gymnastics.

Princess Zora loves to swim.

Princess Zora loves to play with her "Internet Computer."

Princess Zora loves to
watch cartoons.

Princess Zora loves her mom and dad,
Queen Zuri and King Zev.

...And she loves her whole, **entire family** too!

But there is something very special
about Princess Zora...

She's got
a lightning touch!!!
SCHOOL
SCHOOL

Princess Zora's mom
and dad did not know
about her special gift until
they were dropping her off
at Kindergarten one morning.

Princess Zora skipped across the carpet floor in her classroom and leapt into her parents' arms.

Just as she
made contact,
she shocked
her parents
with her
lightning touch!

King Zev and Queen Zuri jumped for joy
when they felt that first shock.

Since that day, every time
Princess Zora skips across any carpet,
she activates her special gift.

She activates her
lightning touch!

And do you know what her
lightning touch is made of?

It's made of
LOVE!

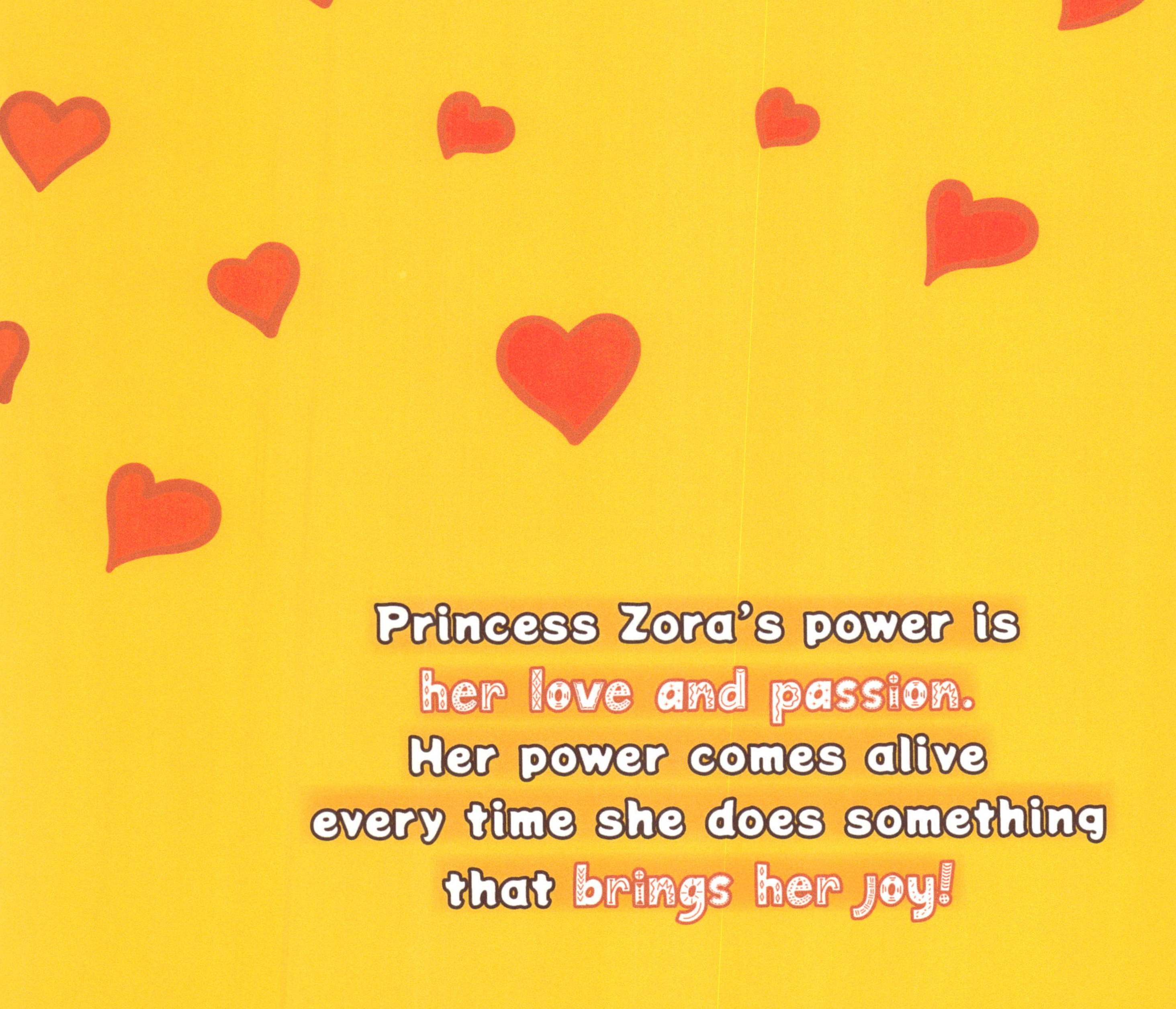

Princess Zora's power is
her love and passion.
Her power comes alive
every time she does something
that brings her joy!

Be passionate about what you love,
and love what you are
passionate about.

The end!

ABOUT THE AUTHOR

Dr. Anthony, better known as **CC Anthony**, is a university professor, entrepreneur, and mentor for women returning to college and the workforce. She works as a lead faculty member and teaches finance, economics, hospitality, and business courses. She has a Bachelor's in Culinary Arts and Hospitality Management, a Master of Science in Finance, a Master of Science in Education, a Doctor of Management in Organizational Leadership, and she is currently working on a Doctor of Philosophy in Education, Instructional Design for Online Learning. For fun, she works out at her local CrossFit gym and runs distance races (including the Marine Corps Marathon and several half marathons) for the "race bling." She also builds websites, creates ads and other graphics and materials for small business owners, and advises small business owners as a consultant. Most importantly, she is a wife and mom, and her **Zora series** is based loosely on the life and experiences of her brilliant and beautiful daughter.

The main character, **Zora**, is named after **Zora Neale Hurston**, author, playwright, anthropologist, higher education professional, and filmmaker.
To learn more about Zora Neale Hurston, please visit the Official Website of Zora Neale Hurston: https://www.zoranealehurston.com/.

Author's website: www.cecilyanthony.com
Contact: drcecilyanthony@gmail.com
LinkedIn: https://www.linkedin.com/in/cecilyanthony/

www.ingramcontent.com/pod-product-compliance
Lightning Source LLC
Chambersburg PA
CBHW042203030726
47602CB00007B/107